How The Moon Stays Afloat

Jasmine Koper

BookLeaf Publishing

India | USA | UK

Presentation by *BookLeaf Publishing*

Web: www.bookleafpub.com

E-mail: info@bookleafpub.com

ISBN: 9789358316216

First edition 2023

DEDICATION

This book is dedicated to the universe which has so graciously allowed me to exist within its contents.

ACKNOWLEDGEMENT

I would like to acknowledge all famous poets and their enviously creative and cunning ways with words that I have never read, but shall try to imitate. I would also like to acknowledge those in my life who inspire me every day (you know who you are), and of course, Joel Deane, because I am really only publishing this book so I can tell you that I'm a published poet.

PREFACE

Welcome to "How The Moon Stays Afloat". In this book, you'll embark on a poetic journey through the eyes of an astronomer who readily confesses to possessing more knowledge of celestial bodies than the nuances of verse. With this admission, you are invited to keep your expectations pleasantly modest as you leaf through these pages.

This collection is a testament to the poet's exploration of the poetic craft, and it reflects a (not so) intimate relationship with words that is both humble and honest. Expect to encounter verses that range from the musings of the sky (a specialty of mine), to reflections on what it is to be human and to experience as many emotions as there are stars in the sky.

In this poetic odyssey, you are encouraged to shed any preconceived notions and embrace the unexpected. You may find that, within the our astronomical poet's words, there lies a universe of enjoyment and insight.

So, dear reader, fasten your seatbelt and prepare to embark on a journey filled with playful metaphors, poignant musings, and a touch of celestial wonder. Let these words transport you to the whimsical, profound, and everything in between.

Tim

There's a dinosaur in my backyard,
his name is Tim.
He holds the secrets of the universe,
and sometimes my sandwiches.
And on a rainy day,
he lets me sit near him,
and snuggle into his feathers for warmth.
But then he must return to the dirt,
and my sandwiches are in my hands,
and the secrets are in the stars.
But things are still alright,
because I know he's still there,
just a few feet down.

Car Rides

In the amber glow of twilight on a long and
winding road,
memories whisper softly, a distant tune hums
gently,
a soft breeze flows through the open window.
I am transported, I am five years old once more.

Laying motionless in the back seat of the car,
The road long, yet sleep has evaded me still.
Eyes remain closed, ears listening
to the quiet conversation and soft radio tunes
kept so, that I may stay in my peace a little
longer.

And when the car hums over that last bump,
slowing into a gentle roll, I squeeze my eyes
shut
as tight as they can be, let my body go limp.
The most convincing feign that I'm still asleep.

Gently, my parents lift me, carry me to my bed,
tucking me in, a whispered goodnight and a kiss.
We both knew the charade, the game we'd play,
forever grateful I never surrendered to the
dreams.

The sun is slipping through the horizon's grasp,
through the window, its warmth quietly departs,
and slowly, oh so slowly, night takes its hold.
In this moment, memories and dreams intertwine
like sand.

I have a long drive ahead, the radio's turned
down.
I cannot lay and sleep, I must be vigilant and
numb,
unsure if the one who'll carry me from my seat
will guide me to my bed, or a place I'll never
return.

Nonsense

4

There's something strangely profound about nonsense.
It just doesn't make sense.

The Tree

5

There's a small tree over the mountain.
It has fruit sometimes,
but whenever I find myself there,
it seems someone picked them all off.
Maybe there never were any fruit.
Is it even a fruit bearing tree?
I'm sure I saw some on it one time,
so why are they never there when I am?

Letter to a Teenage Girl

Chipped butterfly clip
stuck in home bleached hair.
Don't be so down, kid,
you're too young to care.
Too broke to replace the converse
you've had since you were 12,
laces frayed and torn
they sit upon your shelf.
Memories to be cherished,
now waiting to be erased.
The choked desolation
lays clear upon your gaze.
Of teen desperation,
for something more than this;
to come of age,
to feel the joy
of life's lonely bliss.

Amateur

My art isn't for museums or galleries or sales.
It's for sketchbooks, and small gifts.
It's for sharing with friends, for hanging in
hallways,
or sitting in someone's back pocket.

Her voice isn't for stages or albums.
It's for karaoke in the car,
drunken late night singalongs.
It's for singing in showers and while making
breakfast.
It's lullabies and camp songs,
and gentle ballads to loved ones.

His cooking isn't for a Michelin star restaurant.
It's for parties and gatherings
and the absolute best home cooked meals.
It's an extra reason for more time spent
with family and friends.
It's for making any Friday feel like a first date.

Her athleticism isn't for the track, field or court.
It's for making it to the train stop just on time.
It's for carrying all the shopping in one go.
It's for winning every arm wrestle

and beating everyone up flights of stairs
without getting out of breath.

Their dancing it's for the stage or camera.
It's for car parks and bedrooms and clubs.
It's for beating everyone in just dance.
It's for bring rhythm to everything they do.

Your talent is not for the stars.
It's for friends, for family, for yourself.
It's for having fun, making memories.
It's for doing what you love,
because there'll always be someone
waiting to appreciate it.

Lost Letters

Today I learnt
that 14.4 million letters
are lost in the mail every day.
How many birthdays
have been missed?
How many lovers
have been pissed?
How many thank you's,
and get wells,
and goodbyes;
how many caring words
never found the right eyes?

I think of these letters,
words forever stuck in purgatory.
Maybe I'll search for them,
read them all,
but I think it'd bore me.
Sure, there'd be fascinating things,
but most meant for
known eyes,
known hands,
known skin.
It would make no sense to me,
but perfect to those it's meant for.

14.4 million puzzles,
none but few who can decipher.

Indescribable

She was capricious,
like wildfire spreading through dry grass.
She was vivacious,
like the smile shared between old friends.
She was effulgent,
like the midsummer sun radiating on field of
tulips.
She was ineffable,
like the vastness of the sky on a clear night.
She was herself,
but no words the thesaurus can give me
will be enough to show you what that was like.

Longing for Life's Embrace

One day I will no more long for the cold, tender
earth,
and instead I will yearn for the delicate breeze
through a willow tree onto my face,
and ache for the vibrant hues
of summer's sunset bruise against the clouds,
and crave the relief of a warm home
with a fire and a poem on a bitter winter's day,
and pine for the ocean's hold
on my soft body as I float,
watching the evening sky
lose its light slowly,
but surely,
with the certainty that it will come back
again.

Summer

In the summer
as the earth mourns the rain,
the green turns to ochre,
a chromatic tinge adorns the air.
And I am reminded,
briefly,
of a strange nostalgia
for a chrome tinted childhood,
playful and carefree,
that only comes around
in the summer.

Breaking in a Friend

When you get a new friend,
you have to break them in
like a pair of good shoes.
When they're new they're stiff,
the silences are uncomfortable.
The leather of their faces
hard and unyielding.

You just have to keep wearing them in,
and slowly they soften.
The creases begin to appear
near their eyes as their mouths widen.
They soften, just like their expression,
when they see it's you
who's at their door at this hour.
The silences become comfortable
and they mould them-self to you,
as you do to them.

Your inside jokes and shared experiences
wear a you-shaped thing in their lives.
And once you've broken them in,
they'll fit just right.
They'll only get better from here,
and soon enough their voice

will be as familiar
as the pair of shoes on your feet.

guilt

a thousand "sorry"s will never be enough
so i'll stack another brick on my shoulders.
the fault will only ever lie with me
so i'll just paint my filthy hands red.

and i'll scrub your hands clean
until they bleed and are as red as mine.
and then you'll help me lift another brick
as my aching back begins to crumble.

i don't think i can do this much longer.

Sirens of the Night

The great empty sings its songs to me .
each night it calls for my bones.
A melody so sweet, but I will not be
the ulysses to these sirens, no.

I will let the night wash me away,
let it swallow me whole.
Tender arms reach out as I pray
that I'll never be alone.

Like Icarus I'll climb higher and high,
but no sunlight will let me down.
So into the speckled abyss I will fly,
and into the void I will drown.

Comfort in the the eternal embrace,
of an unyielding night.
The everything-nothing's holy grace
holds my aching heart so tight.

But the songs waive and wither,
and fade into the dawn.
No melody to take me hither
and no me to mourn.

So please stay with me, my love,
keep the night as my foe.
Let us ponder as we gaze above,
how the moon stays afloat.

An Ode to Lilac

The twilight sky and its many mysteries,
A colour ever-changing,
Never quite landing on one.
For the briefest moment,
It will fade to the perfect shade.
Blink, and you'll miss it.
But keep your eyes open, and you'll see it,
A color as warm as a crackling hearth,
Yet as cool as a winter's ocean.
The colour of a light breeze, of the feel of silk,
The colour of a brief hug, of a dreaming face.
It'll entice you in its trance and hold you for a
moment,
And then the sky will change, as it always does,
And you'll think of it from time to time.

Bug Catcher

I look up at the stars tonight,
a thousand tiny spots.
Like a thousand little
pin prick holes,
in a small garden pot.
Maybe I'm just a little bug,
with some leaves
and a touch of dirt.
Maybe we're all just little bugs,
in a pot the size of Earth.

Aphrodite

Mother of mothers,
Lover of lovers,
Your glow outshines
The morning sun who
Makes even the clouds blush.
A tremor in the mountains,
A ripple across the land,
The mountains move for you.

But you, oh, Aphrodite, you're not just,
You're the anguish of unrequited love,
The bitter poison of desires unmet,
You are the dark, the sorrow, the abyss,
An abyss that swallows love,
Drowning it in the depths of despair,
Turning desire into desperation.

Mother of mothers,
Lover of lovers,
You may outshine the sun's futile glow,
But in this relentless world,
Where love is both our salvation and doom,
You too are but a puppet of fate,
Dancing in a masquerade of shattered hearts.

Butterflies

There's butterflies in my stomach
but their wings are made of razors.
They tear up my flesh
every time that we touch.
Your hands, dipped in acid
corrode my skin 'til I see bone.
Hold your hand to my chest
maybe then I'll finally see my heart.

Coffee.

The world is burning
Flaming tyres in a pile
Fifteen hundred metres tall
I haven't seen you in a while

The world is in chaos
Pitchforks in the air
People hanging in the streets
I miss that shirt you used to wear

The world is smouldering
Rivers scorched and sterile
Forests reduced to barren plains
Of course I like your new style

The world is collapsing
Anarchy consumes every street
Skies burn with crimson rage
Perhaps soon we could meet

The world is disintegrating
Cities crumbling down
The darkness, it prevails
I'm sure there's something open in town

The world is unraveling
Mother nature's final plea
Time slipping through our grasp
Maybe we can grab some coffee?

An Update.

Each day I am becoming more and more unhinged. As I loosen my tethers to the material world, the expectations placed upon me, and I embrace chaos in its utter beauty, I think I am regaining some of that happiness I've so dearly missed. I am deciding to not exist as a person, but as an entity, a thing. Not to say I'm beyond any of these mortal things, but I think we're so focused on mortality that we ignore so much of the beauty of the world. There's a certain kind of madness that comes with the simultaneity of accepting the horrors of the Earth and the universe, but still choosing to love. The bliss of the ignorance of our childhoods granted us this similar chaotic positivity about life, and it's a feeling so many will keep chasing, but I don't think it's something you can chase. Only embrace a new form of it in full awareness but with a fuller heart, so that you may regain a fuller zest for life. I've always liked the idea of optimistic nihilism. I may be a silly little puppet playing its part in some grand scheme or lack thereof, but I'm going to hold my own strings and do my dance as I please.

Close

Laying in your embrace,
Your skin on my skin,
This contact isn't enough.
Let me open up your chest,
And crawl right in.
What's the point of all these organs,
When I could fit perfectly instead?
Let your warmth be mine,
Let me hear the thoughts,
Running through your head.
I'd feel your heart beat with mine,
Our blood will course together,
As your lungs fill with air,
I'll inhale so deeply,
So we may never
Be apart.
And still,
Still it won't be close enough.

I Miss You.

Oh how you would love this day
The sky is almost blue
The flowers are almost budding
The sun is almost bright
I've got a pair of shoes I don't fit
They would be just your size
Wouldn't you love to wear them?
We could take a walk together
Talk about how things are
And admire the mundanity of life
Perhaps we can dress up as fairies
Wings adorned and glitter everywhere
Like we did when we were young
I haven't seen you in so long
But sometimes you find me again
Just outside of my peripheral
You'll come to visit for a little while
And bring me puddles to stomp in
Like we did when we were young
But the puddles are of my own tears
And my shoes just don't fit
And it's no fun when you're not here
Come again, won't you?
The shoes are just your size,
I'm sure you'd love them.